WOULD YOU RATHER CHALLENGE GAME

VACATION EDITION

Game Rules

1. Find at least two players.
2. Choose a person to ask a question.
3. The other person will choose between the two choices and give a reason why.
4. They must choose an answer!
(No "I Don't Know" or "Pass" or "Both"!)
5. If the person asking the question likes their answer, the person gets a point.
6. Next, the other person gets to ask a question.
7. Keep going until the winner gets 10 points.

If more people play, either assign a judge or have people vote for their favorite answer.

Have fun!

Would you rather wade in a river with your entire luggage or walk one mile to a crossing if a bridge was out?

Would you rather stay on the first floor of an apartment building with noisy neighbors or a quiet 20th floor in a building with no elevator?

Would you rather always wear sunglasses or always wear a hat?

Would you rather hire someone to cook on your vacation or clean up after you?

Would you rather spend the night in a tiny house or a glass house?

Would you rather always wait in long lines for rides at an amusement park or go when half the rides aren't working?

Would you rather always have to walk in wet socks or have your shoes too tight when sightseeing?

Would you rather go on vacation with someone who has lots of money or someone who always agrees with you?

Would you rather road trip to a cold football game or a hot baseball game?

Would you rather spend evenings watching sunsets or spend morning watching sunrises on vacation?

Would you rather get to where you're going by helicopter or by jetpack?

Would you rather be kept up at night by loud music or by a baby crying while staying in a hotel?

Would you rather hold a snake on vacation or get kissed by a camel?

Would you rather share a toothbrush with a family member or use a stranger's pillow on vacation?

Would you rather vacation in a tiny apartment in the busy city or in a large mansion one hour away from everything?

Would you rather always be a little too hot or a little too cold on vacation?

Would you rather travel to the moon in 3 days or take a whole year and travel to Mars?

Would you rather go snorkeling near a reef or hang gliding?

Would you rather always have to wear a clown nose or a clown wig in another country?

Would you rather have no Internet or no air conditioning and heating on a trip?

Would you rather have to eat clams or squid in Spain?

Would you rather do a boat cruise or visit a zoo on vacation?

Would you rather go to the movies or play cards if it was raining on vacation?

Would you rather be stranded on a desert island or be stranded in the mountains?

Would you rather have to milk a cow or brush a horse if you were staying on a farm?

Would you rather vacation as an amazing photographer in Africa or an amazing writer in Australia?

Would you rather spend one year sailing around the world or one year visiting all the state capitals?

Would you rather have too much sand in your shoes or too much sand in your hair?

Would you rather drink milk or drink lemonade for every meal while on a trip?

Would you rather go on the vacation of a lifetime or get the fastest computer ever?

Would you rather be a lifeguard or a waiter for tourists?

Would you rather visit the International Space Station for a week or stay at Sea World for a week?

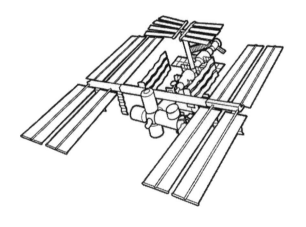

Would you rather vacation in a grass hut on a beach or in a pop-up camper?

Would you rather watch a rocket launch or a Super Bowl game on vacation?

Would you rather take a vacation to Moscow or Manitoba?

Would you rather swim with baby sharks or water snakes on vacation?

Would you rather have Mexican food or Chinese food on vacation?

Would you rather always be too busy or always feel a little lazy on a trip?

Would you rather always take cold showers or never get enough sleep on vacation?

Would you rather go skiing in the mountains or rock climbing?

Would you rather go on a vacation to a sandy white beach or a hotel with five pools?

Would you rather be completely alone for part of your vacation or never alone?

Would you rather live where you are right now for the rest of your life or move to another country?

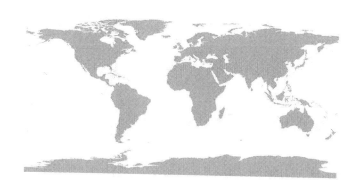

Would you rather go parachuting or bungee jumping on vacation?

Would you rather always smell rotten meat or always smell skunk when visiting a new city?

Would you rather lose all your keys or lose your phone on vacation?

Would you rather set up camp in a remote area or an area with lots of other people?

Would you rather find a mouse in a drawer or a big spider in the bathroom of a hotel?

Would you rather have no Winter Break or have no Spring Break?

Would you rather be on an airplane between two arguing passengers or next to a woman with a growling dog?

Would you rather take a hot air balloon ride or a dune buggy ride on vacation?

Would you rather tour a prehistoric cave or a mummy's tomb on vacation?

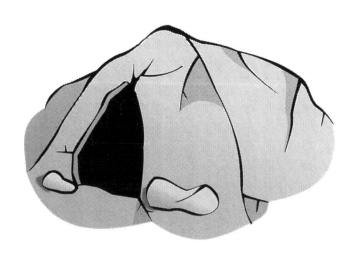

Would you rather lose all your clothes or your tablet on vacation?

Would you rather vacation in a luxury apartment at the top of a skyscraper or a fancy tree house?

Would you rather have to eat snails or rabbit in France?

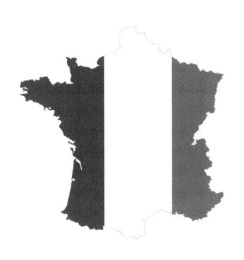

Would you rather never have to brush your teeth or never have to take a bath or shower on vacation?

Would you rather be on vacation on a boat in the middle of the ocean or in a raft the middle of the wild river?

Would you rather get everywhere by an electric scooter or by hover board in a city you didn't know?

Would you rather go on vacation with the president or Lady Gaga?

Would you rather vacation on a houseboat or in an RV?

Would you rather catch frogs or skip rocks on vacation?

Would you rather have a water balloon fight or a pillow fight on your hotel floor on vacation?

Would you rather camp at Yellowstone National Park or at the bottom of the Grand Canyon?

Would you rather vacation in New York City or Hollywood?

Would you rather visit Narnia or the Hogwarts School for a vacation?

Would you rather be a museum guide or a park ranger for tourists?

Would you rather listen to holiday music or your parent's favorite music on a long car ride?

Would you rather get a new pair of shoes or a jacket for vacation?

Would you rather have a submarine ride or a space shuttle ride on vacation?

Would you rather always eat at McDonald's or always have a country's surprise food while on vacation?

Would you rather ride around a city in a convertible or a double-decker bus?

Would you rather go to Antarctica or the Sahara desert for free?

Would you rather
go a whole vacation
without any screen
time or without any
sweets?

Would you rather take the vacation of your life before the age of twenty-one or after the age of twenty-one?

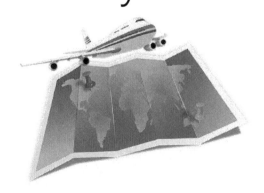

Would you rather relax in a pool of marshmallows or a pool of cotton candy?

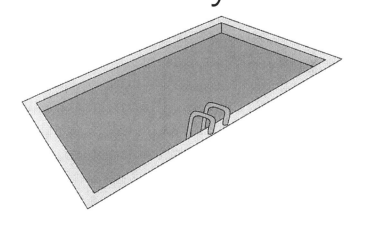

Would you rather be a toll booth worker or a flight attendant?

Would you rather be able stay in an underwater hotel or an outer-space hotel?

Would you rather go fishing or hiking at a beautiful lake?

Would you rather ride a reindeer or an ostrich on vacation?

Would you rather wear clothes that clash or clothes that are out of style while in another country?

Would you rather have 8 younger brothers with you on vacation or travel with only you parents?

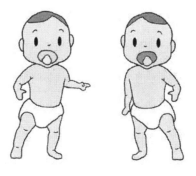

Would you rather ride on an old pirate ship or a speed boat for the day?

Would you rather travel first class on an airplane or first class on a high-speed train?

Would you rather go a pet shop or a bookstore on vacation?

Would you rather have to visit a doctor or lose your luggage while on vacation?

Would you rather travel to the top of a building in a see-through elevator or take a long motorcycle ride?

Would you rather travel the country in an old school bus or a rusty old station wagon?

Would you rather camp in a very cold tent or a warmer tent that is being rained on?

Would you rather take a vacation to a resort island or go visit the Eiffel Tower?

Would you rather go on vacation to a new country every summer or get an extra month of summer break?

Would you rather experience a crazy water slide or a crazy zip line on vacation?

Would you rather take swimming lessons in a cold pool or the ocean while on vacation?

Would you rather have no sense of smell or smell everything around you with extra ability if you were in another country?

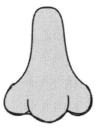

Would you rather be accidentally locked inside a museum or locked a White House bathroom while on vacation?

Would you rather always be an hour early or always be 15 minutes late to where you need to be?

Would you rather travel back in time 100 years or travel to the future 100 years?

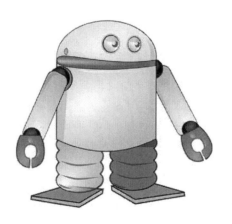

Would you rather be able to read any foreign language or speak any foreign language?

Would you rather discover a buried treasure or see a pride of lions while on vacation?

Would you rather take a vacation without running water or electricity?

Make up your own Would You Rather... to add to the book!

_____

_____

_____

_____

_____

_____

_____

_____

Make up your own
Would You Rather...
to add to the book!

_____

_____

_____

_____

_____

_____

_____

_____

Make up your own
Would You Rather...
to add to the book!

_____

_____

_____

_____

_____

_____

_____

_____

Make up your own
Would You Rather...
to add to the book!

_____

_____

_____

_____

_____

_____

_____

_____

Make up your own
Would You Rather...
to add to the book!

_____

_____

_____

_____

_____

_____

_____

_____

Make up your own
Would You Rather...
to add to the book!

_____

_____

_____

_____

_____

_____

_____